ColourScene
The Vehicles of
East Kent and Maidstone & District
1970 – 1985

N. J. Eadon-Clarke

DTS
Publishing

Published: 2005
ISBN: 1-900515-11-3
Published by DTS Publishing, PO Box 105, Croydon, UK
Printed by Unwin Brothers, Old Woking
© N. J.Eadon-Clarke 2005

www.BooksDTS.co.uk

COVER ILLUSTRATION: A busy scene at Rye Station with M&D 5623 in full NBC livery, compared with the traditional M&D livery this 1963 Leyland Atlantean with Weymann Highbridge body now looks remarkably plain; it is working a service transferred from East Kent in March 1973. **August 1973**

FRONTISPIECE: This 1963 Maidstone & District Leyland Atlantean is part of the dedicated M&D Private Hire fleet hence its renumbering into the 2xxx series. It has a Weymann H44/33F body; 2621 is seen at the village green in Benenden. **18 May 1985**

BELOW: East Kent Daimler Fleetline RFN969G had been on loan to Maidstone & District since November 1978 and would remain so until the end of 1980. Accordingly it has gained its fleetnumber on the front dome to allow its identification by the cameras in the Pentagon bus station. It is seen here approaching the entrance ramp. **1 July 1979**

BACK COVER: Former East Kent 1959 full front AEC Regent V PFN852 is seen as a training bus with Derby City Transport. The M&D and East Kent Bus Club arranged for this vehicle to be on display during a club trip to the area. Clearly blue suits the vehicle almost as much as the original maroon. **28 September 1985**

ColourScene
The Vehicles of
East Kent and Maidstone & District
1970 – 1985
Foreword

My interest in buses began on arrival at secondary school in 1967 where I discovered a flourishing transport society. The core membership devoted their time to railways, but a significant minority were also interested in buses. From the start I took photographs and the easiest way then to take colour shots was to take slides. It is hard to believe 38 years later that in those days colour prints were in comparison to slides very expensive and storage of prints and negatives was a problem not least because it necessitated buying albums and finding a system to store negatives. The difficulty with slides was to get the correct exposure; unlike prints where there was the opportunity to make corrections during the processing with slides it was a case of 'just one chance' and it could be right or wrong. Cameras with built in light meters were rare and even if available were outside the price range of a school boy. Films came with a basic instruction sheet giving a guide as the exposure depending on the weather conditions, basically describing the conditions as 'overcast' or 'sunny with weak shadows' or 'bright sun with sharp shadows'. In consequence it was easier to get the exposure wrong than it was to get it absolutely correct and I can well remember walking around with a separate light meter in an attempt to get better results. Inevitably I have more poor photos from the early years than good ones which is very frustrating when selecting photographs for this book because the memory is better than the quality of the photograph.

In addition to the difficulties explained above was the problem of transport. I didn't pass my driving test and buy my first car until 1977 so visits to the operating territory of Maidstone & District and East Kent relied upon public transport or persuasion of my parents or those of friends to take me on a trip or stop while we were en route for a day trip somewhere else – I was not always very popular!. In consequence many of the photographs in this book, particularly in the early years are taken in or near the garages, however they are no less interesting for that since unlike the situation in 2005 when vehicles are worked hard and must be on the road earning revenue many vehicles particularly the older stock were to be found in garages at weekends or being stored awaiting sale in the yards outside.

East Kent Road Car Company Ltd was formed in 1916; by 1970 the majority of the fleet consisted of products by AEC. Double deckers being AEC Regents introduced from 1959 and single deckers by AEC Reliances. 1969 had seen the delivery of 20 Daimler Fleetlines, but no more new double deckers would be received until a batch of 15 Leyland Atlanteans and 6 Bristol VRTs arrived in 1976. Further batches of Bristol VRTs were delivered until 1981. Following the Reliances thirty seven AEC Swifts were purchased for single decker requirements until the early 70s when the Leyland National arrived in large numbers.

The Maidstone & District Motor Services Ltd was formed in 1911; by 1970 the double deck fleet was dominated by Leyland Atlanteans and Daimler Fleetlines whilst the single deckers were mostly AEC Reliances; the shorter versions of which were gradually being replaced by Leyland Leopards although there had been three batches of Leyland Panthers delivered between 1965 and 1968. From the mid seventies the majority of new deliveries were Leyland Nationals or Bristol VRTs although the company was also the recipient of small numbers of other types for evaluation on behalf of the National Bus Company

During the time covered by this book both companies worked very closely together and vehicle loans between them were common. In 1981 the M&D Head Office in Maidstone closed and the management of both companies was carried out from Canterbury, but in 1983 they separated again. Until 1977 East Kent never used fleet numbers and vehicles were identified by the numbers in the registration plate, however increasing computerisation caused the introduction of a four digit numbering scheme that avoided duplication with that already in operation by M&D. Thus East Kent vehicles used 1xxx for single deck buses, 7xxx for double deck buses and 8xxx for coaches. M&D generally using 2xxx for dual purpose buses, 3xxx for single deck buses, 4xxx for coaches, 5xxx and 6xxx for double deck buses. Both companies had large numbers of coaches for tour work and express services between the main operating centres and London.

I have used various publications published by The M&D and East Kent Bus Club for details in this book and accordingly wish to record my thanks for their permission to do so. Membership of the club is highly recommended and details may be found on page 96. In addition I am eternally grateful to Mike Davis of DTS Publishing who has provided much help particularly with regards to content and layout and everything else needed to enable this book to reach the book shelves. Finally, thanks to Nicholas King for proof reading the final version and making suggestions which I have incorporated where possible.

I hope you enjoy this collection of East Kent and Maidstone & District vehicles which illustrates an interesting period when they worked so closely together.

Nigel Eadon-Clarke
Chislehurst
Kent UK
May 2005

RIGHT: East Kent GJG639D an AEC Reliance with Park Royal C49F body new in 1966 picks up passengers in Eltham High Street whilst working the London to Ramsgate service L1. **3 August 1970**

RIGHT: Delivered in 1956 as DH476 this AEC Regent V with Park Royal body was re-numbered by Maidstone & District as 5476 in 1968. This was one of M&D's only highbridge batch of Regent Vs before the switch to rear engined double deckers in 1959. Seen here in the lower shed used by M&D at Ashford, it would be withdrawn at the end of the year. **2 September 1970**

BELOW: Remarkable survivors with Maidstone & District were three AEC Regals new in 1946/7. They survived by being converted to open top to operate a round the town tour in Hastings; which was a rare conversion for a single decker. Indeed all three still survive in 2005. Here we see 8002 inside one of the sheds of Hastings Brook Street garage. **4 August 1971**

ABOVE: Seen in Skyways livery on the A20 at New Eltham is East Kent AEC Reliance coach GJG643D. **13 May 1972**

LEFT: This smart line of East Kent Beadle bodied AEC Reliance coaches is standing in Ramsgate (Thanet) garage, the front coach is MJG48; the batch of 12 was delivered in 1957. **2 July 1972**

BELOW: Also in Ramsgate garage on this day is DJG614C a 1965 AEC Reliance coach carrying Hoverlloyd livery next to a 'standard' East Kent double decker AEC Regent V WFN827 delivered as the first of the batch new in 1961. **2 July 1972**

5

ABOVE LEFT: The scene inside M&D's garage at Maidstone showing two Harrington bodied AEC Reliances 3369 (408DKK) of 1959 in dual purpose livery together with 3699 a 1963 Reliance in standard fleet livery and specially built to 7ft 6in width for use at Hastings. **July 1972**

ABOVE RIGHT: In 1967 East Kent received a batch of ten Bedford VAS 1 buses with Marshall B29F bodies. Some were converted into Executive coaches, but here standard KJG106E is seen in Dover working a contract to the Tilmanstone colliery. **23 August 1972**

ABOVE: East Kent used, Pencester Road Dover as a parking area and here Bedford VAS1 KJG106E stands next to MJG291 a 1957 AEC Reliance with Beadle DP41F body. **23 August 1972**

LEFT: Inside M&D Silverhill Hastings garage and 1959 Leyland Atlantean 6444 has just become one of the first double deckers to be repainted into NBC grass green. This bus carries a Weymann L39/34F body. After sale by M&D this bus would see further service with Orpington & District and is pictured with them later in this book. **September 1972**

ABOVE LEFT: M&D Leyland Atlantean 6445 is being prepared for repainting inside Silverhill Hastings garage. It can be seen that the roof was the first part to receive the new NBC grass green colour and that repainting was carried out by hand brushing. **September 1972**

ABOVE RIGHT: Traditional liveried vehicles in Silverhill Hastings garage with NBC liveried Leyland Atlantean 6444 at the rear. **September 1972**

LEFT: M&D 3442 seen when three months old outside Silverhill Hastings garage. This was the second in the batch of 35 similar Leyland Leopards with Marshall B45F bodywork and the early members of this batch were the last single deckers delivered in traditional M&D livery; the later examples being delivered in NBC green. **September 1972**

LOWER LEFT: The running shed at M&D's Gillingham garage before it was converted into a maintenance area. The last of the relatively rare batch of dual doored single deck Daimler Fleetlines 3830 with Marshall B45+21D body stands next to 5506 a 1959 Metro-Cammell bodied Leyland Atlantean. The Fleetline was delivered in 1970 and such was its unpopularity it was sold for further use to Alder Valley in 1974. **September 1972**

TOP LEFT: Faversham sees East Kent NFN343 in its twilight years it is a 1957 AEC Reliance with Beadle DP41F body converted to permit one person operation. **September 1972**

LEFT: M&D Leyland Leopard 3457 is seen in Maidstone garage on completion of its delivery run. This was the first M&D single-decker to be delivered new in NBC livery and the fleetname would be applied locally after delivery. **11 November 1972**

LEFT: This cramped scene in Maidstone garage shows on the right the application of the NBC fleetname to a vehicle in traditional livery. On the left is 3762 now in bus livery retaining the M&D scroll fleetname. This was one of two AEC Reliances delivered in 1963 as dual purpose vehicle and has a Willowbrook body. After sale by M&D this was bought by The M&D and East Kent Bus Club as a vehicle for club tours and is illustrated in this role later in this book. **11 November 1972**

LEFT: East Kent Leyland National EFN161L seen in Canterbury Bus Station on trials before entering passenger service still carrying its vehicle identification number 286 in the blind display. The contrast between this new vehicle and the Regent V and Beadle bodied coach alongside is noteworthy. **2 January 1973**

TOP LEFT: This view taken into the winter sun shows brand new East Kent Leyland Nationals in the yard of Canterbury Works. Leyland Nationals carried their vehicle identification numbers (VIN) in the blind display when delivered; EFN160L and EFN162L carrying VIN 285 and 287 respectively. To the left of the photo is part of EFN161L which was being used for initial trials. **2 January 1973**

TOP RIGHT: This is East Kent CFN127 a 1947 Dennis Lancet 3 with a body by Park Royal parked out of use in Herne Bay garage yard, having been converted to full-front with a forward OMO entrance in 1959. It had survived this long due to it being used as an office until at least 1971. **2 January 1973**

ABOVE LEFT: M&D 3344 is a 1961 AEC Reliance with a Weymann body. It is seen here after withdrawal outside Hastings Silverhill garage. A couple of months later it would pass to Wombwell Diesel Co for scrapping. **16 April 1973**

ABOVE RIGHT: In a surprise move M&D acquired five Bristol MW6G with ECW bodies from United Automobile Services, Darlington in December 1972. This rather dark view shows the first 7011HN in store inside Hastings Silverhill garage shortly before repainting when it would became M&D 4701. **16 April 1973**

LEFT: M&D Recovery AEC Regal lorry P32 was rebuilt into this form in 1956 having been delivered with a Harrington bus body in 1937; seen in the corner of Hastings Brook Street garage. **16 April 1973**

BELOW: This view in Maidstone Lower Stone Street bus station illustrates a dual purpose coach of M&D and an East Kent bus. Both buses carry Marshall bodies the M&D vehicle is a AEC Reliance, whereas the East Kent bus is an AEC Swift. The M&D bus carries NBC fleetnames, but the East Kent vehicle has yet to succumb. **18 April 1973**

LEFT: The first Leyland National for Maidstone & District is seen here at the entrance to Tunbridge Wells garage for inspection before entering service. Delivered as 501 it would be renumbered 3501 the following month. **18 April 1973**

CENTRE LEFT: This slightly over exposed picture shows the first All Over Advertisement bus for M&D (Kent Frozen Foods). It is 5595 a 1963 Leyland Atlantean with Weymann highbridge body; note the display includes the offside illuminated advertisement panel. It is working route 98 in Tunbridge Wells. **18 April 1973**

LEFT: East Kent had two batches of AEC Reliance coaches dedicated to touring work bought in 1964 and 1970. The first of the latter batch UFN480H is parked in Ashford garage showing the original very smart traditional livery with italicised fleet name. **27 April 1973**

TOP LEFT: M&D acquired some Duple Dominant bodied Ford R1014 coaches in 1974. Here M&D 4133 is less than one month old when visiting the LT Gala Day at Syon Park. The coach carries NBC white coach livery with the abbreviated fleetname of 'Maidstone'. This coach was sold after only five years use by M&D. **19 May 1974**

TOP RIGHT: The East Kent excursion vehicle to the LT Gala Day at Syon Park was AEC Reliance Plaxton Panorama VFN39H which still did not carry NBC livery or fleetnames. **19 May 1974**

ABOVE LEFT: Standing alongside a Leyland National in NBC Poppy red outside Canterbury Works is 1953 East Kent Guy Arab IV GFN927 with a Park Royal body in traditional livery and TFN437 a 1960 AEC Reliance in Poppy red. **25 May 1974**

ABOVE RIGHT: East Kent EFN184L was numerically the last of the initial batch of 26 Leyland Nationals for the Company. Showing a 'Pay on Entry – Exact Fares Please' notice and side adverts it stands in the yard of Canterbury Works. **25 May 1974**

LEFT: Recently re-instated as cover for other defective vehicles East Kent AEC Regent V PFN880 contrasts traditional livery with the Poppy red colours of adjacent Regents in Canterbury garage yard. This bus was from the first batch of Regent Vs for East Kent built in 1959 and the only East Kent batch to receive full fronts; in the author's opinion the best looking Regents ever made. **25 May 1974**

ABOVE LEFT: Broadstairs Sea Front is the location for this view of East Kent AEC Regent V YJG818 working from Ramsgate (Thanet) garage on Birchington/Ramsgate/Margate/Broadstairs route 50. This was delivered as part of the 1962 batch of seventeen. Traditional livery has been superseded by NBC Poppy red which makes the vehicle appear plain. **25 May 1974**

ABOVE RIGHT: Seventeen years old and still going strong is East Kent MJG47 a 1957 AEC Reliance with Beadle C41C (centre entrance) body. The coach carries a white NBC fleetname and revised livery which contrasts badly with the traditional livery shown earlier in this book. It is parked in Ramsgate (Thanet) garage. **25 May 1974**

CENTRE LEFT: Several members of the 1959 batch of AEC Regent Vs had their service lives extended by being converted to open top by East Kent to replace FFN registered Guy Arabs used hitherto on coastal route 69 during the summer months. Two such vehicles PFN870 and PFN873 stand in Ramsgate (Thanet) garage ready for this role. A couple of Guy Arabs can be seen parked behind. **25 May 1974**

LEFT: The yard outside Ramsgate (Thanet) garage sees East Kent RFN959G still in traditional livery. This is a 1969 Daimler Fleetline with Park Royal body and widely considered to be amongst the most handsome Daimler Fleetlines ever built; this is without doubt enhanced by the smart livery application. **25 May 1974**

LEFT: A number of M&D single deck Daimler Fleetlines were loaned to East Kent in the summer of 1974. Here M&D 3824 is working for East Kent at Folkestone and is taking on passengers in the town bus station. **30 August 1974**

BELOW: East Kent Leyland National EFN169L outside Folkestone bus station. This stop is still used for National Express services in 2005, but behind the vehicle there is now a multi storey office block and car park and the cars are rather different. **30 August 1974**

BOTTOM: Folkestone town services were mostly in the hands of ex Southdown Leyland Leopards with Regent Vs used in the peaks. However there were four AEC Reliances used on the country routes as illustrated here in the bus station by OFN710F on route 90. **30 August 1974**

ABOVE LEFT: In 1971 a batch of 30 Leyland Leopards was acquired by East Kent from Southdown and they were all initially allocated to Folkestone garage. Here 101CUF demonstrates the smart East Kent livery in the town bus station. **30 August 1974**

ABOVE RIGHT: 1956 Weymann bodied AEC Reliance LJG310 is in its final year with East Kent, it is in Folkestone bus station alongside an AEC Regent V in NBC livery. **30 August 1974**

CENTRE LEFT: Another former Southdown Leyland Leopard now with East Kent at Folkestone is 271AUF entering the bus station while working on service 105 to Lydd. **30 August 1974**

LEFT: Whilst the Leyland Atlantean is synonymous with M&D fleet, it is often forgotten that they operated over 100 Daimler Fleetlines (both double and single deck). Here M&D Fleetline 6075 with a Northern Counties LD44/33F body delivered in 1963 as DL75 drops off passengers in Folkestone after its journey from Maidstone. This bus lasted with M&D until 1981 giving it a respectable life of 18 years service. **30 August 1974**

ABOVE: East Kent was a regular operator of re-bodied vehicles. In 1972/3 the 1962 batch of AEC Reliances delivered with Park Royal coach bodies were fitted with new Plaxton Panorama Elite II or III bodies. Here we find 524FN with its new Elite II body in Folkestone bus station prior to its journey to London Victoria coach station. **30 August 1974**

ABOVE RIGHT: East Kent KJG109E is a Bedford VAS 1 fitted with a Marshall B29F body seen here in NBC poppy red livery in Folkestone bus station. **30 August 1974**

CENTRE RIGHT: After a period of hire, four 1961 vintage M&D Leyland Atlanteans were sold to East Kent in June 1974. Here 571RKJ based at Ashford garage waits in Folkestone bus station before its trip to Maidstone on route 10 which was a joint M&D and East Kent route. **30 August 1974**

RIGHT: East Kent used the garage at Hospital Hill, Seabrook, Folkestone, built on the site og the former Sangate railway station as a base for the coach fleet as well as winter storage and a base for the storage of withdrawn vehicles. Here withdrawn Guy Arab GFN928 in open top livery awaits its fate. **30 August 1974**

ABOVE LEFT: Another withdrawn vehicle awaiting sale at the Folkestone, Seabrook garage is 1955 AEC Reliance / Weymann DP41F bus KFN248. **30 August 1974**

ABOVE RIGHT: Cheriton was the home to the Folkestone based bus fleet. TFN425 wearing NBC Poppy red livery stands in the yard. This bus was from the 1960 delivery of AEC Reliances and was built to a dual purpose specification (coach seats in a bus body). **30 August 1974**

CENTRE LEFT: This line up of East Kent Regent Vs is seen in the corner of the Cheriton yard, from left to right are GJD742D of 1966, YJG822 of 1962 and GJG755D also of 1966. Note that that the 1966 vintage Regents carry 'Pay on Entry' notices whilst YJG822 is not converted to operate without a conductor. **30 August 1974**

LEFT: Old and new liveries on Regent Vs of East Kent seen in the Cheriton yard. The older bus YJG820 carries the new NBC Poppy red livery whilst GJG736D remains in traditional colours. **30 August 1974**

TOP LEFT: East Kent AEC Reliance 529FN carries a new Plaxton Panorama Elite III body and a non-NBC colour Scheme with Fleetname in NBC style but without the double N symbol. Compare this with the photo of re-bodied 524FN seen earlier. It is parked in the entrance to Cheriton garage in Folkestone. **30 August 1974**

TOP RIGHT: This Harrington Grenadier coach bodied AEC Reliance of Maidstone & District was numbered 4153. Given its registration: 3294D it always had something of a mystical air about it. Seen here outside Hawkhurst garage in NBC white with abbreviated fleetname it is showing its age because all over white does not complement the curved lines of the bodywork. **18 July 1976**

ABOVE: 1959 East Kent Regent V PFN864 has found a new home with Theobalds Coaches of Long Melford in Suffolk in whose yard it is seen. The livery application well suits the classic lines of the vehicle. **25 August 1975**

LEFT: M&D acquired four AEC Regent Vs from East Kent in June 1974 in exchange for four RKJ registered Leyland Atlanteans. This bus PFN861 numbered 7861 was used for only a short time as a driver trainer in September 1975 at Gillingham garage where it is seen. It was later re-numbered to 5861 and withdrawn in 1976. **September 1975** (*N. J. Eadon-Clarke Collection*)

17

ABOVE LEFT: In the corner of Hastings garage is 4003 one of the two remaining 1946/7 AEC Regals (HKL836) the other being HKL826. it can be seen that it cost 25p to enjoy a Round The Town tour. Parked next to it is M&D 2554 a dual purpose bodied AEC Reliance of 1965 in Dual Purpose NBC livery. **18 July 1976**

ABOVE RIGHT: Also in Hastings garage is 1972 Leyland Leopard / Marshall B45F 3448 in NBC green livery. Compare the look of this vehicle with a similar bus in traditional livery pictured earlier (Sept 72) in this book. **18 July 1976**

LEFT: In 1974 this 1962 AEC Reliance with Weymann body (325NKT) was converted to open top and renumbered 8004, it was later again renumbered 4004. The conversion was unusual in that the bus retained its front dome and full size side and rear windows. Indeed it would be more accurate to say it had its roof removed. This unique vehicle is standing in Hastings Brook Street garage. **18 July 1976**

LEFT: Maidstone & District Leyland National 3532 seen in Hastings when just under one year old. This bus would only serve M&D for 9 years before being sold. **18 July 1976**

BELOW: Maidstone & District was chosen by the NBC to evaluate the new generation of double deck buses. In 1975 it received 5 examples each of the new MCW Metropolitan and Volvo Ailsa. The first base for the comparison of the Metropolitans and Ailsas was Hastings. Metropolitan 5253 is seen here operating in Hastings. **18 July 1976**

RIGHT: Two M&D training buses at Hastings Silverhill garage. P2 (NKT878) is a 1951 Leyland Titan and P3 (VKR469) is a 1956 AEC Regent V. **18 July 1976**

LEFT: Ex East Kent AEC Regent V PFN865 in the process of being converted into a towing lorry for Maidstone & District inside Hastings Silverhill garage. This vehicle still exists as a preserved vehicle in 2005. **18 July 1976**

LEFT: East Kent 1937 Leyland Tiger TS8 (JG9938) in store in Hastings Silverhill garage. This vehicle has survived since it was converted into a mobile office after withdrawal from passenger service. The side roof boards proclaim this to be the Freedom Ticket bus. This bus is now preserved in Somerset. **18 July 1976**

RIGHT: Withdrawn M&D 3269 a 1959 AEC Reliance and the last of the batch awaits its sale in the yard of Hastings Silverhill yard. **18 July 1976**

ABOVE: 1976 was notable as being an exceptionally hot summer. As a result there were complaints of unacceptable heat in the cabs of the five experimental Volvo Ailsas, which are of course front engined. As a result all five were taken out of service until cab ventilation could be improved. Here all five await modifications at Hastings Silverhill garage. **18 July 1976**

LEFT: Maidstone & District short Leyland National 3541 was only one month old when seen inside the garage at Rye railway station. **18 July 1976**

BELOW: East Kent received a batch of 15 Leyland Atlanteans with the less common ECW bodies in 1976. Here JJG15P is seen when new at New Romney. **18 July 1976**

LEFT: As well as trialling the Metropolitans and Ailsas Maidstone & District were also evaluating the VRT with both the Gardner 6LX and Leyland 501 engine. This bus 5106 intended to be part of this trial was not actually included, but was one of the first series 3 VRTs built to full height for M&D. It stands here in the yard of Tenterden garage. **18 July 1976**

BELOW LEFT: UKN207 is actually originally UKN210 and was one of several Harrington-Commers that passed to Simonds of Botesdale for further operation. It had been new in 1955 and is seen here in their yard at Diss Norfolk still in use 21 years later. It would pass into preservation later in 1976 and regain its original registration before being used as a source of spare parts in 1987 and disappearing in 1991. **5 August 1976**

BELOW: Another Harrington-Commer in the fleet of Simmonds of Botesdale at Diss was UKN203. Unfortunately this bus was scrapped in 1983 having given a very creditable 28 years service. **5 August 1976**

BOTTOM: These two East Kent Leyland Nationals (SJG337N and NFN66M) are pictured outside the lower shed at Ashford garage. 337 is a 10m bus whereas 66 is the longer 11m. **15 August 1976**

ABOVE: The front yard of the East Kent garage at Ashford sees three smartly turned out Leyland Nationals. GFN543/7N are 10 metre examples, but older NFN75M is an 11 metre bus. **15 August 1976**

ABOVE: In 1976 the majority of double deckers in the East Kent fleet remained Park Royal bodied Regent Vs. Inside Ashford garage these are represented by faded WFN830 dating from 1961 and AFN770B from 1964. Alongside is the first of the four special Bristol LHS6Ls GFN559N which were specially built as 7' 8" wide and 9' 6" high. **15 August 1976**

ABOVE: East Kent touring coach UFN483H a 1970 AEC Reliance / Duple Commander IV has now been repainted white and is seen with other coaches in Folkestone Seabrook garage. Compare this livery with that shown earlier in this book (April 1973) on a similar vehicle. **15 August 1976**

BELOW: A variety of types in the yard of Folkestone garage including Leyland National EFN163L, ECW bodied Atlanteans JJG11, 9 & 14P, Regent V GJG757D and Towing bus 1951 Guy Arab III FFN381. **15 August 1976**

ABOVE LEFT: Both East Kent and Maidstone & District received some Ford R1014 / Plaxton Derwent B43F buses in 1976. Here is an East Kent example KFN328P the first of the batch seen at Dover Pencester Road. **15 August 1976**

ABOVE RIGHT: Withdrawn AEC Reliances awaiting sale behind Deal garage, TFN438 and WFN504 both carry Park Royal Dual Purpose bodies and AFN602B (far right) has a full specification coach body. **15 August 1976**

LEFT: This scene inside Deal garage shows vehicles that were replacing the withdrawn AEC Reliances parked outside. An unidentified Leyland National is next to a Ford /Derwent KFN330P and AEC Reliance / Dominant C51F HFN30L. **15 August 1976**

LEFT: The sun streams through the roof lights of Deal garage to illuminate this fine line up of Regent Vs. From left to right are GJG737 / 735D, MFN945 / 947 / 942 / 948 / 938 / 949F and GJG746D. **15 August 1976**

23

LEFT: Inside the East Kent garage at Ramsgate (Thanet) and 1959 AEC Regent V PFN855 shows its open top livery and side adverts for summer coastal route 69. **15 August 1976**

RIGHT: This is East Kent 1967 AEC Regent V MFN946F seen inside Ramsgate (Thanet) garage in a livery to advertise its role as a mobile office to issue Freedom Tickets for which role it toured all parts of the East Kent and Maidstone & District operating area. It also meant that it survived longer than its peers and happily is now a heritage vehicle and restored to traditional livery with Stagecoach East Kent. **15 August 1976**

LEFT: A line of three ECW bodied Leyland Atlanteans in East Kent's Ramsgate (Thanet) garage JJG1P heads the line and behind this is JJG5P with JJG6P bringing up the rear. **15 August 1976**

RIGHT: Repainted East Kent Daimler Fleetline RFN960G and new Ford / Plaxton Derwent KFN334P stand inside Ramsgate (Thanet) garage.
15 August 1976

BELOW: 1960 vintage AEC Reliances TFN431 and TFN439 in the yard of East Kent Herne Bay garage, note the roof mounted boat rack on TFN431.
15 August 1976

ABOVE: EK999 is a 1954 Scammell six-wheel recovery unit acquired from the MOD (Army) in 1974. The size of this vehicle can be judged by reference to the cars and coach beside it.
15 August 1976

LEFT: This line of East Kent 1960/1 AEC Reliances is seen opposite Canterbury garage. Visible are WFN501, WFN518 and WFN511. Note that WFN511 carries NBC dual purpose livery.
15 August 1976

ABOVE: East Kent Open Tender BJG421 is a 1945 Guy Arab II seen withdrawn in the yard of Canterbury works. **15 August 1976**

ABOVE RIGHT: The yard of East Kent's Canterbury works finds withdrawn tree lopper BJG461 which had previously operated as an open top bus on coastal route 69 and touring coaches AFN495 / 499B. **15 August 1976**

RIGHT: Compare these two East Kent vehicles in the Canterbury works yard. ECW bodied Leyland Atlantean JJG7P of 1976 stands next to AEC Regent V MFN952F of 1967. **15 August 1976**

LEFT: East Kent executive coach Bedford VAS1 KJG 108E stands next to Touring AEC Reliance coach UFN486H outside Canterbury works. **15 August 1976**

ABOVE LEFT: We have already seen an example of the East Kent Ford R1014 / Plaxton Derwent buses, here is the Maidstone & District version, 3266 in the rain at Sheerness bus station. **31 August 1976**

ABOVE RIGHT: Next out of Sheerness bus station is 1965 AEC Reliance / Marshall B53F now numbered 3714 after sale two years later this bus was exported to Jamaica. **31 August 1976**

LEFT: Maidstone & District acquired this 1961 AEC Regent V from East Kent for use as a training bus. WFN835 is now numbered P4 in the service vehicle fleet. It is about to leave a rainy Sheerness bus station. **31 August 1976**

BELOW: Maidstone & District Gillingham garage sees full height 1963 Leyland Atlantean 5622 next to lowbridge 1963 Daimler Fleetline 6077 and 1965 AEC Reliance 2557 the last of the batch wearing dual purpose livery. **31 August 1976**

ABOVE: In 1972 Maidstone & District exchanged 12 single deck Fleetlines for 12 double deck Fleetlines from Northern General. Here 5007 a 1969 Fleetline with Alexander H44/33F body leaves Chatham Pentagon bus station. The large fleetnumber on the front dome was to allow the bus station roof mounted cameras to identify vehicles entering and leaving the bus station. This bus appears again later in this book in a non psv role. **31 August 1976**

ABOVE RIGHT: In 1976 Maidstone & district received a batch of 7 Leyland Leopards with Duple Dominant C47F bodies. 4140 is outside the traffic office at Gillingham garage. Particularly noteworthy are the alternate red and blue seats and the abbreviated fleetname 'Maidstone'. **24 October 1976**

CENTRE RIGHT: During the re-building of the Maidstone & District garage at Bexhill vehicles were parked on the forecourt of the former Bexhill West railway station opposite. Here we find Leyland Panther / Strachans B48F 3132 next to Ford R1014 / Plaxton Derwent B43F 3268. Just visible behind is the last lowbridge Leyland Atlantean in the fleet 6449. Happily, 3132 survives in preservation. **21 November 1976**

LOWER RIGHT: Hastings town centre and Maidstone & District Metropolitan 5251 is about to be passed by Leyland Leopard 3457 in an all over advertisement livery for Ward's. **21 November 1976**

ABOVE LEFT: Harrington bodied coaches survived long enough in the Maidstone & District fleet to receive National white livery. These two withdrawn examples (22TKR and 26TKR) stand awaiting sale outside Hastings Silverhill garage. **21 November 1976**

ABOVE: Standing in the corner of Hastings Silverhill garage is training bus P5 in the Maidstone & District service vehicle fleet it is former East Kent Regent V YJG814. **21 November 1976**

CENTRE LEFT: Rebuilding work is taking place at Hastings Silverhill garage behind two vehicles being trialled on behalf of NBC. Metropolitan 5253 is next to Ailsa 5384. **21 November 1976**

LEFT: On 5/5/74 Maidstone & District bought the business of John Dengate & Sons of Rye and with the business acquired eight vehicles. Two former Dengate Leyland Leopards are seen here inside Rye Station Road garage. On the left is Leyland Leopard 2852 with Willowbrook DP49F body and next to it is 2854 a similar Leyland Leopard, but with a Plaxton Elite Express III DP53F body. **21 November 1976**

RIGHT: East Kent opened a new bus garage in Ashford at the Cobbs Wood Industrial Estate and inside we find the last vehicle in the fleet to wear the traditional livery 1960 AEC reliance TFN429. It is parked next to 1964 vintage AEC Regent V AFN769B. **21 November 1976**

CENTRE RIGHT: East Kent VJG198J is an AEC Swift with Marshall B51F body delivered at the end of 1970. It is parked outside the new garage at Ashford Cobbs Wood. **21 November 1976**

BELOW LEFT: GFN559N is one of the 'special' Bristol LHS6L's delivered in 1975, it is working route 507 when caught by the camera in Station Road Ashford. **21 November 1976**

BELOW RIGHT: Maidstone & District single deck variety in Sittingbourne garage. Three Leyland Nationals share the yard with a Willowbrook bodied Leyland Panther, single deck Daimler Fleetline (3818) and Leyland Leopard Coach 4111. **21 November 1976**

LEFT: Happily this bus still exists in preserved form. Maidstone & District training bus P1 (NKT875) a 1951 vintage Leyland Titan outside Sittingbourne garage, the vehicle behind is 1962 Harrington Cavalier bodied AEC Reliance 23TKR. **21 November 1976**

ABOVE: This 10m Leyland National (3531) was just over one year old when photographed in the yard of Sittingbourne garage. **21 November 1976**

LEFT: Maidstone District Leyland Atlantean 6444 was pictured earlier in this book (September 1972) just after painting into NBC green. Here it is seen after sale to Orpington & District in May 1975 at their Green St Green garage which subsequently became the home of Metrobus. **3 January 1977**

LEFT: Maidstone & District Bristol VRT 5803 from their first batch of VRTs wore this all over advertisement livery for London and Manchester Assurance for 3 years. It is parked inside Tunbridge Wells garage. **1 May 1977**

LEFT: Outside Station Road Ashford garage and East Kent Leyland National EFN160L shares the yard with AEC Swift / Marshall B51F RJG203G both looking extremely smart. **8 May 1977**

BELOW LEFT: East Kent Leyland National MFN118R a 1976 delivery stands of the forecourt of the new garage at Cobbs Wood Ashford. **8 May 1977**

BELOW: The yard of Folkestone Cheriton garage sees ECW bodied Atlantean JJG11P and Leyland National NFN67M. **8 May 1977**

BOTTOM: Inside the new garage at Cobbs Wood Ashford, two former Maidstone & District Leyland Atlanteans 571RKJ and 575RKJ are parked behind JG9938 the 1937 Leyland Tiger TS8 office pictured earlier in this book. **8 May 1977**

LEFT: 1962 vintage AEC Regent YJG812 in faded poppy red livery stands in the East Kent Folkestone garage amongst Leyland Nationals. **8 May 1977**

CENTRE LEFT: Looking in fine shape despite being 11 years old is East Kent GJG632D the first of the 1966 batch of AEC Reliances with Park Royal C49F body stands outside Folkestone Seabrook garage. **8 May 1977**

BELOW LEFT: Also still going strong were this pair of 1964 AEC Reliance touring coaches AFN488B and AFN494B, the glass in the roof cove panels can be seen in this view at Folkestone Seabrook garage. **8 May 1977**

BELOW: In 1971 East Kent received a batch of Alexander bodied AEC Swifts which were mainly associated with Dover garage. Here YJG585K stands at the entrance of Dover garage. **8 May 1977**

ABOVE LEFT: This 1953 Guy Arab IV GFN928 had been retired from its duties as a training bus, but was still used as a towing vehicle when seen here parked at Dover Pencester Road. **8 May 1977**

ABOVE RIGHT: East Kent Regent V GJG747D received this livery for P & O Normandy Ferries for use between Dover and Dover Docks. It passes the P & O offices in this view. **8 May 1977**

CENTRE RIGHT: This 1974 AEC Reliance / Duple Dominant C51F is a former East Kent vehicle. It is now in the ownership of National Travel South East when caught outside Ramsgate (Thanet) garage in Hoverlloyd livery. **8 May 1977**

RIGHT: East Kent full front AEC Regent V PFN855 is being used for driver training duties before the summer open top service commenced when seen inside Ramsgate (Thanet) garage. **8 May 1977**

LEFT: These two AEC Reliance coaches parked outside Ramsgate (Thanet) garage demonstrate the application of the NBC white coach livery. OJG133F has a Willowbrook C49F body and older DJG629C has a Park Royal body. **8 May 1977**

BELOW: These withdrawn East Kent vehicles were awaiting disposal in the yard of Herne Bay garage. WFN839 is a 1961 AEC Regent and the two AEC Reliance coaches are AFN598B and AFN599B all have Park Royal bodies. **8 May 1977**

BELOW LEFT: Also at Herne Bay garage awaiting sale was this Bedford VAS1 KJG112E which had been an executive coach with East Kent, the vehicle behind it is AEC Regent V YJG813. **8 May 1977**

BELOW RIGHT: Brand new and yet to be licensed for service by East Kent is this Ford R1014 / Plaxton Derwent B43F NFN326R waiting for its final checks in Canterbury Works yard. **8 May 1977**

LEFT: The yard of East Kent's garage in Canterbury finds AEC Swift VJG195J and AEC Reliance WFN501. **8 May 1977**

BELOW: 11 Metre East Kent Leyland National MFN120R is about to leave Canterbury bus station. **8 May 1977**

BELOW LEFT: Two Maidstone & District vehicles both with route 5 destination blinds at Hawkhurst bus station. On the left is 1968 dual purpose Leyland Leopard with Willowbrook body 2806 and alongside is series 2 Bristol VRT 6686 built to a height of 13' 5" evidenced by the lack of white band on the front above the windscreen. **15 May 1977**

BELOW RIGHT: Maidstone and District received three batches of Leyland Leopard buses between 1970 and 1973. This is 3413 from the first batch with a Marshall B45F body standing in the roadway outside Hastings Silverhill garage. **15 May 1977**

LEFT: Maidstone & District 4003 a 1947 AEC Regal converted to open top in 1958 stands inside Hastings Silverhill garage, new Bristol VRT 5116 is parked behind. **15 May 1977**

RIGHT: The 1970 batch of Leyland Leopard touring coaches were quite difficult to catch in use. Parked between duties opposite the Maidstone & District garage at Bexhill is 4624 which carries a Duple Commander IV C48F body. **15 May 1977**

BELOW: By this date Maidstone & District had only two Harrington Cavalier bodied AEC Reliances still in use. One of the two is illustrated here, 28 TKR (4028) has seats for only 29 and is seen inside Hastings Brook Street garage. **15 May 1977**

RIGHT: Standing outside Rye, South Undercliffe garage which opened in 1932 for East Kent and passed to Maidstone & District in 1973 before closure in 1980 is Maidstone & District dual purpose Leyland Leopard 2801 the first of the batch of 18. **15 May 1977**

BELOW: Spot the differences between these two 1965 Maidstone & District AEC Reliances parked outside Tenterden garage. On the left is 3718 bodied by Marshall and numbered in the 'bus' series. On the right is 2540 bodied by Weymann in the 'dual purpose series', both vehicles would be sold the following year. **15 May 1977**

ABOVE: Also outside Tenterden garage are Maidstone & District AEC Reliance 3743 with Weymann body and recently transferred in from Bexhill Ford R1014 / Plaxton Derwent 3268. The former would survive in the fleet for two more years and the latter would last three further years being sold in 1982. **15 May 1977**

LEFT: This former Northern General Daimler Fleetline (5012) stands outside the Maidstone & District central workshops in Maidstone, known as Postley Works which opened in 1922 and would close in 1983. **15 May 1977**

LEFT: Despite its run down appearance this Maidstone & District Daimler Fleetline would remain in service until 1984. 6082 had been delivered in 1964 so would give 20 years service. It is awaiting attention outside Maidstone Postley works. **15 May 1977**

BELOW LEFT: In the doorway of Maidstone garage is M&D 4157 a Harrington Grenadier bodied AEC Reliance delivered in 1964. The national white livery and fleetname gives no hint that the parent company has a green based livery. **15 May 1977**

BELOW RIGHT: Earlier in this book (April 1973) I illustrated one of these ex United Automobile Services Bristol MW6G still in United colours. Four years later the fourth in the batch Maidstone & District 4704 is seen in Maidstone garage, it would remain in the fleet for another two years. **15 May 1977**

BOTTOM: After operation in Hastings the Maidstone & District Metropolitans and Ailsas moved to the Medway towns for further trials. Volvo Ailsa 5383 is seen in the front yard of Gillingham garage. **15 May 1977**

LEFT: Also in Gillingham garage, but in the adjacent bus station is Maidstone & District Metropolitan 5251. **15 May 1977**

CENTRE. Maidstone & District used three former East Kent AEC Regents as training buses at this time. P4 and P5 have already been illustrated, here is P6 GJG745D standing in Gillingham garage. **15 May 1977**

LEFT: This Maidstone & District Weymann bodied Leyland Atlantean had been delivered in 1963. Fleet No. 5599 would serve the company for 4 more years giving a respectable 18 years service. It is parked in Gillingham garage with other similar vehicles. **15 May 1977**

ABOVE: This line up in the Maidstone & District garage in Chatham (Luton) demonstrates well the varied double deck fleet and their varying heights. From left to right we have 5632 a full height Leyland Atlantean, 6088 a lowbridge Daimler Fleetline, 5385 a full height Volvo Ailsa, 6113 a lowbridge Daimler Fleetline, 5102 a full height Bristol VRT and finally 5007 an ex Northern General full height Daimler Fleetline, 15 May 1977

LEFT: Hastings coach station is the location of Maidstone & District full height Bristol VRT 5116 delivered three months earlier. 5 June 1977

BELOW LEFT: Also in Hastings coach station is this 1968 Leyland Leopard with Duple (Northern) Commander III body numbered 4606. This coach would see further service with Dack (Rosemary Coaches) in Kings Lynn after sale by M&D in 1980. 5 June 1977

BELOW RIGHT: Maidstone & District 5732 is a full height Bristol VRT delivered new in 1975 seen here at Hastings (Silverhill) garage. After sale by Hastings & District this would be one of four vehicles from this batch sold to Eastern Counties for further use in Norwich where their full height required them to carry a distinctive centre band to distinguish their height. 5 June 1977

ABOVE LEFT: This Leyland Panther, Maidstone & District 3035 carries a Willowbrook body and has only one more year to serve M&D. Seen here in Hastings Silverhill garage yard. **5 June 1977**

ABOVE RIGHT: Despite appearances Maidstone & District Leyland Panther 3116 is still in use and would remain so for another two years it is parked in Hastings (Silverhill) garage next to former East Kent Regent V PFN865 whose conversion into a recovery truck for M&D is almost complete. The Panther carries distinctive Strachans Paceline bodywork. **5 June 1977**

CENTRE LEFT: Single deckers at Maidstone & District Tenterden garage. Leyland National 3548 is only a few months old in this view; the AEC Reliances 3743 (left) and 3718) have bodies by Weymann and Marshall respectively; both date from 1965. **5 June 1977**

LOWER LEFT: Tenterden High Street sees Maidstone & District 3264 working route 400 this is a 1976 Ford R1014 with Plaxton Derwent body. **5 June 1977**

ABOVE: These brand new dual purpose Leyland Nationals have yet to enter service and accordingly still display their vehicle Identification numbers (VIN) in the blind box. They are in store in Faversham garage. Maidstone & District allocated fleet numbers 2904 and 2906 to this pair, which were fitted out to suburban coach specification for use on longer routes. **5 June 1977**

CENTRE RIGHT: New earlier in the year is this standard full height Bristol VRT Maidstone & District 5115 seen in the lower maintenance area of Tunbridge Wells garage. **6 June 1977**

RIGHT: Despite the influx of large numbers of Bristol VRTs the early Leyland Atlanteans remained in regular use. Standing outside Gillingham garage is 5622 new in 1963 and 5577 new in 1961. **7 June 1977**

ABOVE: Coaches in the Maidstone & District fleet are represented here outside Gillingham garage by AEC Reliance / Harrington Grenadier 4172 and Leyland Leopard / Duple Commander III 4601; of particular note is that 4172 was the very last Harrington bodied coach received by M&D. **7 June 1977**

ABOVE RIGHT: Earlier in this book (Nov 72) we saw 32YKK in Maidstone garage, here it is again after sale to The M&D and East Kent Bus Club who named it 'The Maid of Kent' and used it to operate club tours. It is parked alongside other preserved vehicles at the Hillingdon Show. **26 June 1977**

RIGHT: This 1964 Daimler Fleetline / Northern Counties is numbered 6061 in the Maidstone & District fleet. It is seen here receiving attention at M&D's central workshops at Postley and it would go on to give five years more service to the company. **23 October 1977**

BELOW LEFT: Maidstone & District ordered twenty Leyland Nationals to suburban coach specification, but diverted delivery of nine examples to East Kent. NFN83R illustrates the type in dual purpose livery outside Ashford Station road garage. **11 December 1977**

BELOW RIGHT: 1977 was the last year that Maidstone & District would receive new Leyland Nationals. This is 3560 from the last batch new three months earlier operating route 10A in Ashford Station road. **11 December 1977**

TOP LEFT: M&D operated three former East Kent Regent Vs as training buses. This view shows that East Kent likewise used Regent Vs in the same role. 1959 AEC Regent PFN863 was re-numbered P150 in their service fleet and it is seen at Folkestone (Cheriton) garage on a damp December day. **11 December 1977**

TOP RIGHT: Showing that an AEC Regent V could look smart in NBC poppy red at least when recently repainted is GJG739D standing in Folkestone bus station. Note the 'pay on entry' notices on the front nearside wing and adjacent to the door. **11 December 1977**

ABOVE LEFT: Service 90 ran between Folkestone and Dover. Here East Kent AEC Reliance / Marshall B53F OFN713F is loading in Folkestone bus station. **11 December 1977**

ABOVE RIGHT: The first of the batch of Alexander bodied AEC Swifts for East Kent YJG581K now numbered 1581 is working in Dover town centre. **11 December 1977**

LEFT ABOVE: East Kent 7005 is an ECW bodied Leyland Atlantean which carries an all over advertisement livery for Rediffusion. It is seen in Folkestone bus station. The Thanet area route number indicates that it has just arrived at Folkestone on transfer. **11 December 1977**

LEFT: Although unpopular with Maidstone & District eight single deck Daimler Fleetlines found a useful home with East Kent on Seaspeed and Sealink contract services linking Dover Priory Railway Station with Dover docks. Their dual doorways being particularly useful for passengers who were carrying luggage. Now numbered 1805 with East Kent SKO805H waits at the railway station. **11 December 1977**

LEFT: East Kent 1333 is from the first batch of Ford R1014 / Plaxton Derwent buses delivered in 1976. It is parked between journeys in Dover Pencester Road. **11 December 1977**

BELOW: Only a short time before it was withdrawn from service 1963 AEC Regent V now numbered 7788 in the East Kent fleet stands outside Dover garage. **11 December 1977**

BOTTOM LEFT: New East Kent Leyland National 1345 (PJJ345S) is waiting for its next duty in Deal bus station. **11 December 1977**

BOTTOM RIGHT: A grey December day in the yard opposite Canterbury garage. New East Kent Leyland National 1342 the first of the 1977 batch shares the space with 1968 AEC Reliance 1718. **11 December 1977**

LEFT: East Kent touring coach HFN58L (8058) an AEC Reliance/ Duple Dominant C42F stands outside Canterbury garage. **11 December 1977**

CENTRE LEFT: Parked in the layover area of Canterbury bus station is one of nine Leyland Nationals delivered in 1977 being their last batch it is East Kent No. 1343. **11 December 1977**

BOTTOM LEFT: Just one week before the Maidstone & District garage at Gravesend closed sees ECW bodied Bristol VRT 5826 built to intermediate height (13' 8") as evidenced by the narrow white band across the windscreen next to a 1973 Leyland National. **25 March 1978**

BOTTOM RIGHT: Maidstone & District Leyland Panther / Willowbrook 3030 (DKE255C) would be sold five months after this view near Gravesend garage one week before local services were transferred to London Country at Northfleet and the garage closed. **25 March 1978**

ABOVE: General view of the Maidstone & District garage at Gravesend one week before closure. Bristol VRT 5827 stands outside looking very lonely. **25 March 1978**

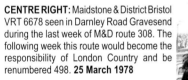

CENTRE RIGHT: Maidstone & District Bristol VRT 6678 seen in Darnley Road Gravesend during the last week of M&D route 308. The following week this route would become the responsibility of London Country and be renumbered 498. **25 March 1978**

RIGHT: Another Maidstone & District route set to disappear with the closure of Gravesend garage would be route 307 to be replaced the following week by London Country route 497. Here M&D VRT 6682 demonstrates the 'old order' at Westmount. **25 March 1978**

LEFT: In addition to the low height VRTs in the HKE...L series Gravesend garage also used mid height ECW bodied VRTs such as 5830 the last of the 1974 batch working on route 308 at its terminus River View Park. **25 March 1978**

CENTRE LEFT: Former East Kent 1951 Guy Arab III FFN379 was converted to open top by East Kent for the summer coastal service in 1969. After sale it passed to Lewingtons of Cranham and is seen here on the outskirts of Brighton on the day of the Historic Commercial Vehicle Club's annual London to Brighton run closely followed by a LT RF. **7 May 1978**

LEFT: PFN882 was the last of the batch of the 1959 delivery of full front Regent Vs. Despite its appearance here it is no longer owned by East Kent. It is in fact being operated by Cavendish Coaches of Eastbourne and was found parked in Brighton on the day of the HCVC London to Brighton Run. **7 May 1978**

ABOVE LEFT: The Maidstone & District batch of Leyland Nationals built to suburban coach specification were used on routes such as this. Route 919 was a part replacement for Green Line route 719 into London. Fleet No. 2905 is seen operating the route in Sidcup High Street. **19 May 1978**

ABOVE RIGHT: After sale by Maidstone and District in April 1978 this AEC Reliance with Harrington Grenadier body (FKL121D) the first of the 1965 batch was one of four that passed to Ebdons of Sidcup. It is standing at Victoria with a former British Airways Atlantean (LLH6K) on Sightseeing duties behind. **30 July 1978**

BELOW LEFT: Former Maidstone & District S210 which has acquired the registration from similar vehicle S207 and is still at work despite being over 22 years old with Simonds of Botesdale as seen here. **12 Aug 1978**

BELOW RIGHT: This former Southdown and East Kent Leyland Leopard 289AUF is standing near Lambeth bridge while in the ownership of Lewingtons of Cranham. **28 August 1978**

RIGHT: East Kent touring coach UFN487H swings into Victoria coach station amongst a sea of other white coaches. **3 September 1978**

LEFT: Folkestone bound East Kent AEC Reliance / Plaxton Panorama Elite I VJG476J – and one of the fairly rare 12 metre examples – prepares to leave Victoria coach station. **3 September 1978**

CENTRE LEFT: Maidstone & District painted one coach in Olau-Line Livery to connect London with the ferry terminal in Sheerness, the coach was 4125 a 1974 AEC Leopard / Duple Dominant C49F seen here in poor lighting inside Victoria coach station. **10 September 1978**

BOTTOM LEFT: This intermediate height Bristol VRT of Maidstone & District (5836) is waiting its next duty outside Tunbridge Wells West railway station. **6 May 1979**

BOTTOM RIGHT: This former Maidstone & District 1954 AEC Reliance / Harrington C37C TKM316 is standing unused in the yard of Goddard at Ightham. Although bought for preservation later in 1979 it was unfortunately stripped for spares and scrapped in 1986. **6 May 1979**

ABOVE LEFT: Speeding down Bromley High Street is Maidstone & District 2811 in dual purpose livery en route to the south coast. **19 May 1979**

ABOVE RIGHT: In 1979 Chatham dockyard held an open day and Maidstone & District were contracted to provide a shuttle bus service. Full height Bristol VRT 5118 waits in the dockyard for its next journey. **28 May 1979**

BELOW LEFT: Happily this former East Kent AEC Reliance with Weymann dual purpose body (KFN220) was subsequently preserved and remains extant in 2005. In this view it is leaving Southchurch Park during the Southend bus rally. **3 June 1979**

BELOW RIGHT: Earlier in this book FFN379 was illustrated with Lewingtons. Here another Lewingtons vehicle from the same batch (FFN384) is also leaving the Southend bus rally with a full load for an open top tour of the locality. **3 June 1979**

RIGHT: After sale by East Kent AEC Reliance touring coach AFN499B found a new home with Thomas of West Ewell. The glass roof panels can be clearly seen in this view in Epsom High Street. **6 June 1979**

ABOVE LEFT: This 1972 Leyland Leopard is numbered 3450 in the Maidstone & District fleet and is seen standing in Maidstone bus station. **1 July 1979**

ABOVE: During the mid 70s there were various vehicle loans between East Kent and Maidstone & District. Here East Kent Daimler Fleetline RFN961G is on loan to M&D as it pulls back from the stand at Maidstone ready for its trip to Tunbridge Wells on route 7. **1 July 1979**

LEFT: This is the Maidstone bus rally and East Kent EFN182 a Guy Arab III / Park Royal L27/26R from 1950 attended to show the restoration work being carried out. This bus had been bought direct from East Kent for preservation as long ago as 1968. **1 July 1979**

LOWER LEFT: This 1963 Leyland Atlantean, 5628 of Maidstone & District is still hard at work 16 years later as seen here in Maidstone bus station where it is about to depart for Chatham. **1 July 1979**

LEFT: Approaching Maidstone bus station is this mid height Bristol VRT 5832 from the 1979 batch. **1 July 1979**

RIGHT: Check the white band on the front of these two Bristol VRTs to get a comparison of the heights and it is obvious in this view at Maidstone & District's Gillingham garage. Full height Bristol VRT 5118 is parked next to intermediate height 5856. **1 July 1979**

LEFT: This Maidstone & District Bristol VRT 5855 is just a couple of months old and still devoid of advertisements when caught by the camera loading in Gillingham bus station. **1 July 1979**

LEFT: Large parts of the Pentagon bus station are fairly dark, but this view of Maidstone & District Metropolitan 5252 is taken between the entrance and exit ramps when there are open sides allowing in the daylight. **1 July 1979**

CENTRE LEFT: New at the beginning of the year is Maidstone & District Duple Dominant I Express bodied Leyland Leopard 2150 which carries dual purpose livery, it leads other NBC white coaches in Southampton Coach station. **3 August 1979**

BELOW LEFT: East Kent 8531 is a 1962 AEC Reliance rebodied in 1973 with a new Plaxton Panorama Elite III coach body. Seen here in Victoria coach station. **18 August 1979**

BELOW: This Bristol LH East Kent 1562 has gained Sealink livery for the shuttle service to the harbour. It is parked in Folkestone bus station. **22 October 1979**

55

LEFT: Also in Folkestone bus station is this former Maidstone & District Leyland Atlantean 575RKJ which is now East Kent 7575 and still looks in good shape bearing in mind that it is approaching its eighteenth birthday. **22 October 1979**

RIGHT: In 1978 East Kent bought five single deck Daimler Fleetlines from PMT to use alongside the eight examples acquired from Maidstone & District on Seaspeed shuttle services at Dover. Here Alexander 'W' bodied BEH153H (1853) is just leaving Dover Priory railway station. **22 October 1979**

BELOW LEFT: Half of the ex Maidstone & District single deck Daimler Fleetlines bought by East Kent carried Sealink livery (the others had Seaspeed livery). Here Sealink liveried 1822 stands next to AEC Regent V GJG735D at Pencester Road Dover. **22 October 1979**

BELOW RIGHT: Working a contract service in Dover is East Kent Regent V GJG752D. **22 October 1979**

ABOVE LEFT: In 1979/80 all NBC companies carried out the 'Market Analysis Project' to match services more closely with demand. East Kent used this 1963 AEC Regent V as a mobile office for the project and re-numbered it P147 in the service vehicle fleet. It is seen at the end of Pencester Road Dover. **22 October 1979**

ABOVE RIGHT: An overcast October day sees East Kent 1971 AEC Swift YJG590K in central Dover. **22 October 1979**

LEFT: Showing that a Willowbrook bodied Bristol VRT was able to pass through the West Gate in Canterbury City centre East Kent 7022 arrives in the city centre. **22 October 1979**

LOWER LEFT: Despite an influx of Leyland Nationals East Kent was still operating a number of AEC Reliances on bus work late in 1979. Here 1968 examples OFN718F and OFN724F are waiting their next duties in Canterbury bus station. **22 October 1979**

ABOVE: The Maidstone & District garage in Sheerness was located in the industrial sounding Power Station Road. It would be closed in January 1981. One year earlier and 5011 one of the twelve Alexander bodied Daimler Fleetlines bought in 1972 stands outside. **4 April 1980**

ABOVE RIGHT: New at the start of 1980 were the first Dennis Dominators for Maidstone & District. This is the first of the batch of six (numbered 5301) and carries a Willowbrook H43/31F body, it is working service 140 opposite Chatham (Luton) garage. **4 April 1980**

CENTRE RIGHT: East Kent route 507 in Ashford has a very low bridge and hence the use of these specially built Bristol LHSs. Fleet number 1559 takes on passengers in Ashford High Street. **18 April 1980**

LOWER RIGHT: Still in use on Ashford Town service 501 is this 1964 AEC Regent V 7770 showing that without external advertisements a Regent V could still look good in NBC Poppy red. **18 April 1980**

ABOVE LEFT: In 1979 East Kent purchased this Ford A0609 bus with Wadham Stringer Voyager B23F body for use on routes to the William Harvey hospital. It is awaiting its next journey outside Ashford Station Road garage. **18 April 1980**

ABOVE: Withdrawals of this OKO...G batch of dual purpose bodied Leyland Leopards commenced in 1980 although this bus (2813) would last until the following year before being sold for scrap. It is working route 297 in Tenterden High Street. **18 April 1980**

CENTRE LEFT: These two M&D Leyland Leopard coaches RKM619 & 620G have been withdrawn and are awaiting sale outside Rye garage. RKM620G would subsequently be purchased by members of The M&D and East Kent Bus Club for use on club tours. **18 April 1980**

LOWER LEFT: This Maidstone & District Bristol VRT 5117 carried this garish overall advertisement for the Deluxe Leisure Centre in Hastings for one year. It stands at Rye railway station awaiting a return trip to Hastings. **18 April 1980**

59

LEFT: This is one of Maidstone & District's 1976 batch of 11 metre Leyland Nationals. 3550 stands at Rye railway station. **18 April 1980**

CENTRE LEFT: Acquired in January 1980 from South Yorkshire PTE was this East Lancs bodied Bristol VRT new in 1972. Renumbered from 5767 to 5784 to match its registration (OWE284K) this bus would provide 7 years service for M&D. It is standing on the outskirts of Hastings. **18 April 1980**

BELOW LEFT: One week before the closure of the Maidstone & District garage at Bexhill and Willowbrook 003 MkII bodied Leyland Leopard 2156 the first of the batch and new in January 1980 stands inside. **18 April 1980**

BELOW RIGHT: It is often the case that a particular vehicle that survives longer than its contemporaries due to a non psv role ends up in preservation. Such is the case with East Kent OFN721F which is now preserved. This 1968 Marshall bodied AEC Reliance is acting as a mobile office for the sale of Freedom tickets in Hastings bus station. **18 April 1980**

ABOVE LEFT: This 1968 Leyland Panther with Strachans body was living on borrowed time when this photograph was taken it being withdrawn shortly afterwards. 3136 is working special OAP contract service B in Hastings. **18 April 1980**

ABOVE RIGHT: Earlier in this book (May 1977) I showed this Maidstone & District Daimler Fleetline awaiting attention outside Maidstone, Postley works. Here it is again in Maidstone bus station on route 155. **25 April 1980**

LEFT: Maidstone & District 6131 is an example from the last batch of double deckers that had been delivered in Traditional livery. It is a Daimler Fleetline with Northern Counties LD44/33F body and was numerically the last of the batch of 20, it is seen approaching Chatham Pentagon bus station on route 166. **25 April 1980**

LOWER LEFT: In 1979 two Leyland Leopards with Duple Dominant II coachwork were diverted from East Kent to Maidstone & District. 4155 was the second of the two and is seen at Gillingham garage. **25 April 1980**

BELOW: Most welcome was the repaint of 1960 Maidstone & District Atlantean 5558 into traditional livery in March 1980 to mark the fiftieth anniversary of the absorption of the Chatham & District company. This photograph taken at Chatham station shows the bus as originally repainted before the cream 'moustache' was added in May. This vehicle is currently preserved and operates internal services within Chatham dockyard. **25 April 1980**

RIGHT: A striking overall advertisement livery is displayed by East Kent Willowbrook bodied VRT 7021. Note the 'key' on the front roof dome. It stands in Canterbury bus station. **24 August 1980**

LEFT: The writing on the building behind these two vehicles shows that this view is opposite the East Kent garage in Canterbury. AEC Regent V 7950 shares the spot with Willowbrook Bristol VRT 7973 the first of the second batch received in 1978. **24 August 1980**

RIGHT: Approaching Broadstairs seafront is another East Kent Willowbrook bodied Bristol VRT, this time it is 7981 on Broadstairs/Ramsgate/Margate service 50. **24 August 1980**

ABOVE: 1980 was the last summer season for the open top East Kent AEC Regents to operate coastal route 69. Here 1959 full front AEC Regent V PFN873 is in Broadstairs High Street. **24 August 1980**

LEFT: Sharing route 50 with Bristol VRTs is this East Kent ECW bodied Leyland Atlantean numbered 7001. It is collecting passengers on Broadstairs sea front. **24 August 1980**

BELOW LEFT: Ex Southdown and East Kent 1963 Leyland Leopard 278AUF has found a new owner in A.P.C. It is parked here outside Ramsgate (Thanet) garage. **24 August 1980**

BELOW: New to East Kent in 1980 was a batch of mid height ECW Bristol VRTs. Represented here by 7650 and 7651 sharing the yard at Ramsgate (Thanet) garage with 1976 Leyland National 1894. **24 August 1980**

ABOVE LEFT: East Kent Leyland National NFN75M has been sold to South Wales and is shown here in course of delivery to them. It has stopped by some shops on the A20 at Crossways New Eltham. The blind display shows the 'Devils' number '666' which may or may not be significant, but is most likely because the vehicle operated at Ashford which used this route number for their Ashford to Faversham service. **3 October 1980**

ABOVE RIGHT: This spot outside the East Kent garage in Station Road Ashford will usually find a red Leyland National on lay-over. This time however we find a green Maidstone & District example 3548. **4 October 1980**

ABOVE LEFT: Earlier in this book (November 1976) I illustrated two vehicles acquired by Maidstone & District with the business of Dengate, Rye. Here is a third vehicle Leyland Leopard / Willowbrook 2853 seen here very smartly turned out in NBC dual purpose livery in Ashford Station Road. **4 October 1980**

ABOVE: East Kent Suburban coach specification Leyland National 1083 in dual purpose livery in Ashford Station Road. **4 October 1980**

LEFT: Recently re-certified Maidstone & District 1973 Leyland Leopard 4107 with Duple Dominant body seen in Folkestone bus station ready for its trip to London Victoria coach station. **4 October 1980**

LEFT: East Kent's Bristol VRTs carried bodies from two manufacturers. 7046 at the front of Folkestone bus station has full height ECW bodywork whereas 7985 behind was bodied by Willowbrook. **4 October 1980**

CENTRE LEFT: This East Kent Bristol VRT 7655 carries intermediate height ECW bodywork as evidenced by the narrow white band above the windscreen. It is about to depart Folkestone bus station on route 555 to New Romney. **4 October 1980**

BELOW LEFT: Leaving Dover Priory railway station is ex PMT single deck Daimler Fleetline 1841 in Seaspeed livery. **4 October 1980**

BELOW RIGHT: New earlier in the year is this intermediate height ECW bodied Bristol VRT 7662 about to leave Dover Pencester Road for the journey to Canterbury. **4 October 1980**

ABOVE: East Kent Leyland National 1080 in its last few weeks with the company seen in Herne Bay High Street on route 647. **4 October 1980**

ABOVE LEFT: Comparison of livery on this Bristol LHS6L 1560 with that on 1562 pictured earlier in October 1979 in the same location will reveal that Sealink livery has been brightened. **4 October 1980**

ABOVE RIGHT: This ex Maidstone & District Leyland Leopard of 1969 was one of several to see further service with Ebdon of Sidcup in whose garage it is seen here. It carries a Duple (Northern) Commander IV C48F body and had been M&D 4615. **29 December 1980**

BELOW LEFT: This former East Kent 1960 AEC Reliance TFN432 turned up at the North Weald bus rally in 1981. **31 May 1981**

BELOW RIGHT: This pair of East Kent Leyland Nationals in Canterbury bus station demonstrate the bus livery on 1339 and dual purpose livery on 1086. **26 July 1981**

LEFT: For the 1981 season East Kent replaced the AEC Regent Vs on coastal route 69 with three fresh open top vehicles, allowing the service to become one man operated. One was a Bristol VRT and two were former Maidstone & District Leyland Atlanteans. One of the latter is seen here on the seafront at Broadstairs. Now numbered 0620 this had been 5620 in the M&D fleet. **26 July 1981**

CENTRE LEFT: In the same spot outside the putting green on Broadstairs seafront is the newly converted Bristol VRT now numbered 0977 with East Kent. This was converted following roof damage. **26 July 1981**

LOWER LEFT: Here is the third bus in Broadstairs, ex Maidstone & District Leyland Atlantean 572RKJ now East Kent 0572 which had been acquired from M&D in 1974 and had previously worked in normal service until roof damage caused this conversion. **26 July 1981**

LEFT: East Kent Willowbrook bodied Bristol VRT 7976 carried this unibus advertisement for the Co-op Westwood Hypermarket which was near its home garage of Ramsgate (Thanet). Passengers are boarding at Broadstairs seafront stop. **26 July 1981**

CENTRE LEFT: An unusually overcast August day greeting the crowds who had booked to ride on three AEC Regents on the occasion of the AEC Regent Farewell Tour staged by East Kent. Here the three Regents (GJG741D from Folkestone and GJG757 & 758D from Ashford) are about to load in Canterbury bus station. **9 August 1981**

BELOW LEFT: The first stop on the AEC Regent Farewell Tour was Ramsgate (Thanet) garage. Parked in the doorway waiting to greet us was Bristol VRT 7651 carrying this all over advertisement livery for excursions and holidays with East Kent and M&D. **9 August 1981**

BELOW RIGHT: Inside Ramsgate (Thanet) garage was privately preserved 1959 full front AEC Regent V PFN874 in the as acquired condition complete with NBC fleetname. This bus is still preserved and has since been restored to traditional livery. **9 August 1981**

RIGHT: After Ramsgate it was on to Dover. This arranged photo stop was to allow AEC Regent GJG741D to be captured in the shadow of the famous White Cliffs, unfortunately the weather has still not improved. **9 August 1981**

CENTRE RIGHT: This former Southdown Fleetline was one of several recently obtained by East Kent in 1981. VUF324K is now 7324 and carries P&O Livery for contract work around Dover where it is seen. **9 August 1981**

BELOW LEFT: East Kent has pressed VUF323K into service without repainting it red, but adding fleetnames to the Southdown green. It stands next to AEC Regent V MFN948F at Pencester Road Dover. **9 August 1981**

BELOW RIGHT: This former Maidstone & District single deck Daimler Fleetline with Marshall B41D body has been in the East Kent fleet for five years. 1817 is standing in the bus parking area of Dover Pencester Road. **9 August 1981**

LEFT: East Kent 7016 is numerically the first Willowbrook bodied Bristol VRT in the East Kent fleet, it is working the 550 service to Hythe when captured on film in Dover. **9 August 1981**

CENTRE LEFT: Here are the three East Kent Regents on the Regent Farewell Tour at the lunch stop in Pencester Road Dover. Notice the vehicles carry 1,2 & 3 in the blind displays. 9 August **1981**

BELOW LEFT: Standing outside the rear shed at Ashford Station Road is East Kent Leyland Atlantean 7571 which was acquired from Maidstone & District in 1974. Hard to believe that this bus is twenty years old and would still give East Kent over two years more service. **9 August 1981**

BELOW RIGHT: Sharing the Ashford yard with the twenty year old Atlantean is brand new Bristol VRT / ECW 7676 specially posed for the cameras of those on the AEC Regent farewell tour. **9 August 1981**

RIGHT: The end of the East Kent AEC Regent farewell tour and the buses returned to Canterbury, here AEC Regent 7741 (GJG741D) on which I travelled pauses at the West Gate for photographers to capture the moment in early evening gloom. **9 August 1981**

BELOW LEFT: Earlier in this book (Aug 75) ex East Kent Regent V PFN864 was pictured in the yard of Theobalds Coaches at Long Melford. By 1981 it had been withdrawn from service for some time as evidenced by the moss on the roof and side panels. It was then parked well away from public gaze in the rural village of Hartest reached via very narrow country lanes. The ex Nottingham Daimler Fleetline parked alongside looks to be in much better condition. **22 August 1981**

BELOW: RIGHT: Former Maidstone & District 4163 (FKL126D) a 1965 AEC Reliance with Harrington Grenadier body is photographed in Chislehurst only a couple of hundred yards from the author's home. It is now with Interland Coaches and on a school run from Kemnal Manor School. The school has long since closed and the site is now a modern housing development. **19 October 1981**

LEFT: In 1972/3 Maidstone & District received twenty Leyland Atlantean 'Specials' diverted from an order of 50 intended for Midland Red (LCBS received the other 30 as AN91-120). The previous month this example 5718 became the second to be converted to coach specification and painted in this distinctive livery for commuter services from the Medway towns to London. The coach seating and antimacassars can be clearly seen in this view outside Gillingham garage. **30 December 1981**

ABOVE LEFT: Maidstone & District training buses at Gillingham garage. 1968 Northern Counties bodied Daimler Fleetline 6115 has become P185 and ex East Kent Regent V 7812 is P142 in the service vehicle fleet. Note that the Fleetline carries both East Kent and M&D fleetnames. **30 December 1981**

ABOVE RIGHT: This 1963 Leyland Atlantean (5632) was the last of the batch. Eighteen years old, but still looking good in Chatham (Luton) garage. This bus would survive another two and a half years before being sold for scrap. **22 May 1982**

RIGHT: In 1982 Maidstone & District & East Kent each acquired some Leyland Leopard / Duple Dominant II coaches from Fox, Hayes. This East Kent example 8424 is standing in the M&D Chatham (Luton) garage yard. **22 May 1982**

BELOW LEFT: A consecutively numbered pair of low height Daimler Fleetlines in the Maidstone & District fleet. 6123 and 6124 parked at the rear of Chatham (Luton) garage. **22 May 1982**

BELOW RIGHT: 1972 built Leyland Atlantean of Maidstone & District (5718) is parked next to 1963 version (5632) in Chatham (Luton) garage. **22 May 1982**

ABOVE LEFT: Single deck training buses were rare in this period. 1970 Leyland Leopard UKE412H was an exception being numbered P187 in the service vehicle fleet. It is seen here at Chatham (Luton) garage. **22 May 1982**

ABOVE RIGHT: The rear yard of Gillingham garage was frequently used to store withdrawn vehicle prior to sale. Leyland Atlanteans 5599 and 5596 await their fate. **22 May 1982**

LEFT: As a prelude of things to come the following year the Maidstone & District operations at Hastings and Rye adopted a new identity. In consequence former South Yorkshire East Lancs bodied Bristol VRT OWE281K has gained new Hastings & District fleetnames in this view outside Gillingham garage paint shop. **22 May 1982**

BELOW LEFT: This former Maidstone & District 2803 has now become P186 in the service vehicle fleet. Its new role is that of a staff bus. It is parked for photographers in Gillingham bus station. **22 May 1982**

BELOW RIGHT: East Kent 8532 a 1962 AEC Reliance with 1972 Plaxton Panorama Elite II body was converted into the Freedom Coach for the Disabled. It is seen here parked in Canterbury garage yard. **22 May 1982**

ABOVE LEFT: A rare visit inside the Canterbury paint shop of East Kent finds former Fox of Hayes Leopard MNK425V being prepared for painting. This would shortly become 8425 in the East Kent fleet. **22 May 1982**

ABOVE: Also seen inside the paint shop of the East Kent workshops in Canterbury is this former Fox of Hayes Leyland Leopard MNK426V which would become East Kent 8426. **22 May 1982**

LEFT: Looking like new and fresh from the paintshop is this former Southdown Daimler Fleetline VUF322K how 7322 in the East Kent fleet standing in the yard opposite Canterbury garage. **22 May 1982**

LEFT: This ECW bodied Bristol VRT (7650) is surrounded by other VRTs bodied by Willowbrook in Canterbury bus station. **22 May 1982**

ABOVE LEFT: This 1976 Ford 1014 / Plaxton Derwent has already been sold by East Kent. The former 1330 has a new role as staff transport for Betteshanger Fruit Farm where it is parked for this photograph. **22 May 1982**

ABOVE RIGHT: In addition to the Ford Derwent the Betteshanger Fruit Farm owned a second former East Kent vehicle in the shape of 1966 AEC Regent V / Park Royal GJG739D also seen at the farm in this view. **22 May 1982**

RIGHT: Maidstone & District Atlantean 5718 in Invictaway livery poses specially for this photograph during a tour by The M&D and East Kent Bus Club. The location is Betteshanger Fruit Farm. **22 May 1982**

RIGHT: Three of the former Southdown Daimler Fleetlines acquired by East Kent in 1981 carried this livery for P & O for work between Dover Docks and the town. Standing in the doorway of Dover garage are East Kent 7324 and 7326. **22 May 1982**

LEFT: Dover Pencester Road is the home for this fine line up of East Kent AEC Regent Vs some nine months after the operation of the Regent farewell tour they are still in use on contract work. **22 May 1982**

CENTRE: Six of the former Southdown Daimler Fleetlines with Northern Counties bodywork acquired by East Kent in 1981 were painted into this attractive Hoverspeed livery. This is 7315 in Dover. **22 May 1982**

LEFT: Dack of Terrington St. Clement trading as Rosemary Coaches acquired two of these former Maidstone & District 1968 Leyland Leopards (former 4606 & 4610). Here NKL210F shows its Duple (Northern) Commander body as it stands in their Kings Lynn yard. **22 July 1982**

RIGHT: East Kent were chosen by NBC to take delivery of the first single deck Metroliner coaches which was attempt by a British company to offer a modern product to compete with increasingly popular European coaches. The result was something like nothing ever seen before. The NBC publicised their launch at Victoria coach station on 7 April 1983 and here 8843 is seen turning into the Coach Station for the event. **7 April 1983**

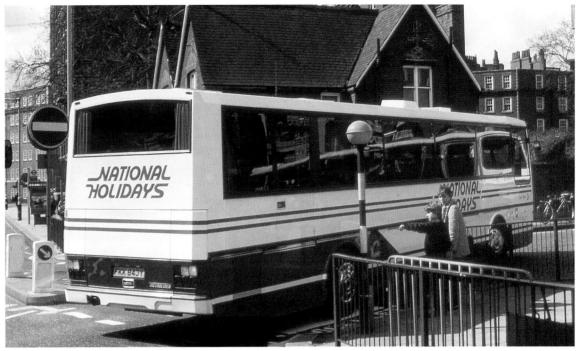

CENTRE: This view at the official handover event at Victoria Coach Station shows East Kent 8845. Note the small East Kent fleetnames under the drivers cab window. The square frontal profile looked modern, but quickly became dated and later deliveries had a more rounded front. **7 April 1983**

RIGHT: East Kent 8843 was used for the 'Official Handover Ceremony' hence the temporary barrier erected around its front inside Victoria Coach Station. **7 April 1983**

ABOVE LEFT: Privately owned former Maidstone & District RKM619G a Leyland Leopard from the batch received in 1969 makes an appearance at the North Weald bus rally, The windscreen sticker reads "Loughton Garage Social and Sports Club". **22 May 1983**

ABOVE RIGHT: Several of the former Dengate vehicles acquired by Maidstone & District have already been illustrated. One that hasn't is 2855 a 1973 Leyland Leopard with dual purpose Paxton Panorama Elite Express III body seen here on express route 900 at Gatwick Airport. **28 May 1983**

LEFT: The last AEC Reliance coach received by East Kent before the switch to Leyland Leopards is this 1975 delivery, GFN558N numbered 8558 is a 12metre coach with a Duple Dominant C55F body. It is loading up in Canterbury bus station for the trip to London. **16 October 1983**

BELOW: Dover Pencester Road and East Kent AEC Swift RJG201G, single deck Daimler Fleetline SKO818H and former Southdown Double deck Daimler Fleetline VUF315K all of which are used for contract work to Dover Docks stand waiting for their next trips. **10 November 1983**

ABOVE LEFT: The parking area at Dover Pencester Road finds East Kent Regent V 7951 alongside former Southdown Daimler Fleetline 7320. **10 November 1983**

ABOVE RIGHT: This former Maidstone & District Marshall bodied Daimler Fleetline is now 1824 in the East Kent fleet, it is seen departing from Dover Priory railway station displaying 'Calais' in the blind box being the destination of potential passengers rather than the bus itself. **10 November 1983**

RIGHT: Sharing the Sealink services with the Daimler Fleetlines is this 1969 Marshall bodied AEC Swift East Kent No.1207. It carries a full load of Calais bound passengers at Dover Priory railway station. **10 November 1983**

LOWER RIGHT: Showing the asymmetrical windscreen a design feature common to all Metro-Cammell-Weymann bodied products of the era and the National Holidays livery application is East Kent touring coach 8846 parked in Canterbury, opposite the bus garage. **10 November 1983**

ABOVE LEFT: Maidstone & District received five long wheelbase ECW coach seated Leyland Olympians for Invictaway commuter services during 1983. Fleet number 5443 stands in Victoria coach station on a gloomy January day. **2 January 1984**

ABOVE RIGHT: New to Maidstone & District the previous December was this ugly Duple Laser bodied Leyland Tiger numbered 2183 seen in Tunbridge Wells High Street en route to London. **26 March 1984**

ABOVE LEFT: Maidstone & District 5031 was one of 20 former London DMS Class Daimler Fleetlines (DMS2090) acquired via Ensign in mid 1982. By the time of this photograph in Gillingham bus station it had been operational for around 12 months and would eventually give M&D 10 years service. **29 March 1984**

ABOVE RIGHT: A vehicle shortage in 1984 caused Maidstone & District to hire various vehicles from a number of sources throughout the year. Four dual purpose seated 11m Leyland National were hired from Crosville Motor Services including this one MLJ957P given temporary M&D number 3957. It is seen at Gillingham garage under the customary cloud of Leyland National blue smoke. **29 March 1984**

LEFT: The East Kent tree lopper P196 (MFN939F) a 1967 AEC Regent V returning to Canterbury works with tree debris on board. **29 March 1984**

ABOVE LEFT: With a unibus advert for Future World Video fully automatic East Kent Bristol VRT 7674 awaits custom in Ashford High Street. **28 April 1984**

ABOVE RIGHT: During 1984 East Kent acquired four 11m Leyland Nationals from London Country Bus Services Ltd. Here NPD141L shows it new fleet number, 1141 and red livery with black bumpers as it turns into Ashford Station Road garage. **28 April 1984**

LEFT: 1984 saw the 25th anniversary of the first Regent Vs bought by East Kent. 7943 one of the few remaining AEC Regent Vs in the fleet was repainted into traditional livery by way of celebration. In this view at Chilham Woolpack the M&D and East Kent Bus Club have hired the vehicle for an anniversary tour. **28 April 1984**

BELOW LEFT: In addition to buying Leyland Nationals from London Country East Kent also acquired examples from Maidstone & District. Here East Kent 1514 (formerly M&D 3514) stands in Herne Bay garage yard. **28 April 1984**

BELOW RIGHT: Evoking many memories and specially posed for this photograph is traditional liveried East Kent Regent V 7943 at the Smugglers Inn in Herne. **28 April 1984**

ABOVE: Former London Transport DMS1672 now Maidstone & District 5022 emerges from Tunbridge Wells garage to take up duty on route 6 to Maidstone. **19 May 1984**

LEFT: Just a couple of months old Maidstone & District Mark2 Metrobus 5203 is working in Tunbridge Wells High Street. M&D had planned that the Metrobus would become its standard new double deck bus, but in the event this role would fall to the Leyland Olympian. **19 May 1984**

BELOW LEFT: Grays Thurrock Civic hall was the venue for a dance troupe competition that brought together a variety of former M&D and East Kent vehicles. River Valley Coaches arrived with a former East Kent AEC Reliance WJG141J. **3 June 1984**

BELOW RIGHT: The Medway Crystallettes acquired former Maidstone & District Marshall bodied AEC Reliance HKT578D also at Grays Thurrock Civic Hall. **3 June 1984**

ABOVE: Also at Grays Thurrock Civic Hall were these two former East Kent vehicles. AEC Swift VJG198J owned by the Twinettes in front of DJG619C an earlier former East Kent AEC Reliance now being used by Thameside Majorettes. **3 June 1984**

ABOVE RIGHT: Looking extremely smart despite being 13 years old is this former East Kent AEC Reliance WJG470J on display at the Southsea rally restored to 'as new' condition. **17 June 1984**

CENTRE RIGHT: This is a survivor from Maidstone & District's only batch of AEC Regent Vs delivered new in 1956. VKR470 is now preserved and is seen on display in Norman Park Bromley during a motor show. **24 June 1984**

RIGHT: Sandringham House coach park is the location for this view of former East Kent 6543FN a 1963 AEC Reliance re-bodied in 1974 and now being operated by Caroline Seagull. **25 July 1984**

ABOVE LEFT: Earlier in this book I illustrated some former M&D Leopards in the yard of Dack at Kings Lynn. A return visit now finds former East Kent 1970 AEC Reliance VJG479J. **26 July 1984**

ABOVE RIGHT: Two more former East Kent Reliances now operating for Caroline Seagull seen outside Norwich castle 6539FN is at the front and the vehicle behind is 6542FN. **27 July 1984**

LEFT: Following fire damage to 2426 Maidstone & District acquired this vehicle as a replacement from Golden Boy of Roydon. XGS771X was numbered 4771 and is wearing NBC coach livery when caught by the camera at Rye railway station. **30 September 1984**

BELOW LEFT: A very wet day finds two Maidstone & District coaches at London Victoria coach station. Leyland Olympian 5445 is seen in Invictaway livery next to Leyland Tiger 2185 in full NBC coach livery now with the company's full name on the front panel. **17 March 1985**

BELOW RIGHT: In 1983/4 East Kent arranged to fit new Berkhof Esprite bodies to a batch of 1973 AEC Reliances. Here 8200 is parked outside London Victoria coach station. This coach had previously been registered HFN58L. **17 March 1985**

LEFT: Just a couple of months old is Maidstone & District ECW bodied Leyland Olympian coach 5446 from the second batch of similar vehicles. It is arriving at Victoria on a wet March day. **17 March 1985**

BELOW LEFT: Over ten years since the acquisition of the business of Dengate of Rye and Leyland Leopard 2852 is still going strong. It would serve Maidstone & District for another year before being sold for scrap. It is parked at the rear entrance to Tunbridge Wells garage. **12 May 1985**

BELOW RIGHT: This 1963 Maidstone & District Leyland Atlantean had just been transferred to the private hire fleet when it was hired for a club trip; in consequence it was renumbered from 5821 to become 2621. It is seen here outside the yard of Wealden at Mereworth next to former East Kent AEC Reliance 6548FN. **18 May 1985**

BELOW LEFT: Happily this former Maidstone & District coach 410FKL still survives in preservation and had at one time been owned by the publisher of this book. It is a 1959 Harrington bodied AEC Reliance 470 and has been moved to allow this photograph to be taken in the yard of Wealden at Mereworth. **18 May 1985**

BELOW RIGHT: New Enterprise Coaches of Tonbridge would be purchased by the owners of Maidstone & District in 1988. Some years before this event the company was operating this former M&D Marshall bodied AEC Reliance HKT580D standing amongst their other stock at Tonbridge. **18 May 1985**

TOP LEFT: After passenger use by both Northern General and Maidstone & District Daimler Fleetline GCN805G formerly 5003 has been converted into a tree lopper and numbered P32 in the service vehicle fleet. It stands at the rear of Tunbridge Wells garage. **18 May 1985**

ABOVE: These two Maidstone & District are working in the private hire fleet as denoted by the sign painting, hence their re-numbering as 2687 and 2621. The Leyland Atlantean is based at Gillingham and the Bristol VRT at Tunbridge Wells; they are posed for the camera outside Tunbridge Wells garage. **18 May 1985**

ABOVE LEFT: Although the operations at Hastings and Rye had become a separate entity (as Hastings & District) in 1983 the majority of vehicles operated in 1985 had come from the Maidstone & District fleet. Included were the two remaining 1946/7 AEC Regals. This vehicle 436 was repainted into the new H&D colours of maroon/cream. It is about to provide a ride to club members in the Hastings Silverhill garage yard. **18 May 1985**

LEFT: Rear view of Hastings & District 436 at Silverhill Hastings garage. **18 May 1985**

LOWER LEFT: The other AEC Regal 426 retained traditional Maidstone & District livery seen at the same location. Notice the canvas roof protection for the drivers cab. **18 May 1985**

RIGHT: Hastings & District adopted a new livery of maroon/cream known as Arrow livery. This open top Bristol VRT 690 carries so called Reverse Arrow livery in that the usual maroon and cream areas have been swapped. It is parked in the garage yard at Silverhill Hastings. **18 May 1985**

BELOW: Hastings & District 165 was formerly M&D 4165. It is a 1980 Leyland Leopard with Duple Dominant II body. It shows off its new H&D livery and logos at Silverhill Hastings garage. **18 May 1985**

ABOVE: This former Maidstone & District Leyland Leopard / Dominant new in 1974 shows how the 'Hastings' fleetname has been applied to NBC coach livery. H&D 116 is also at Silverhill Hastings. **18 May 1985**

LEFT: Hastings & District 268 at Silverhill Hastings shows its new livery of grass green with white roof. This bus had previously been LCBS LNB68. **18 May 1985**

ABOVE LEFT: This ex Ribble Leyland National PTF753L had been the first Leyland National to be converted to a kneeling bus for disabled passengers. Hastings & District acquired it the previous year and it is seen in the Silverhill Hastings workshop alongside another Leyland National in Arrow livery. **18 May 1985**

ABOVE RIGHT: This is the new Hastings & District Arrow livery as applied to a Leyland National, 370 was formerly M&D 3570. It is undergoing attention at Silverhill Hastings. **18 May 1985**

CENTRE LEFT: Many years before Stagecoach would be become a dominant operator along the South Coast this Hastings & District former Maidstone & District Willowbrook 003 MK II Leyland Leopard awaits its next departure at Rye railway station on 'Stagecoach' route 799. It is 156 in the H&D fleet. **18 May 1983**

LEFT: Also at Rye railway station and unlike 268 seen earlier this former LCBS Leyland National does not have a white roof. Numbered LNB39 in LCBS days it is now Hastings & District 239 and sports new H&D fleetnames with the 'arrow' logo on the front. **18 May 1983**

LEFT: A Maidstone & District VRT creeps into this view of the garage at Tenterden. The flat above the Travel Office was for many years owned by Maidstone & District for the use of the General Manager. **18 May 1983**

CENTRE LEFT: This was the first of three ECW Leyland Olympians diverted to Maidstone & District from a Devon General order in 1984. This bus (M&D 5888) arrived already painted in long lasting poppy red and in consequence it was selected to wear this red based all over advertisement for BBC Radio Kent. It approaches the entrance ramp to Chatham Pentagon bus station. **25 May 1985**

CENTRE RIGHT: Also wearing an all over advertisement livery this time for Invicta Sound Maidstone & District ECW bodied Bristol VRT 5855 approaches Chatham Pentagon. **25 May 1985**

LEFT: The third all over advertisement liveried Maidstone & District bus entering Chatham Pentagon is another ECW bodied Bristol VRT, 5109, promoting Gillingham FC. **25 May 1985**

RIGHT: Maidstone & District acquired six new Dennis Dominators with Willowbrook bodies in 1980. In 1983 a seventh vehicle was obtained, but this time with a body by Alexander as seen here leaving Chatham Pentagon bus station. XBF700S was bought from Potteries where it had been No.700. Now it has become M&D 5300. **25 May 1985**

BELOW: Numerically the last of the batch of twenty former London Transport DMS Daimler Fleetlines KUC971P has become Maidstone & District 5040 when captured on film at Chatham Tesco. **25 May 1985**

ABOVE: A club trip to the North East included a visit to OK Motor Services at Bishop Auckland. The company very kindly offered us a ride on former East Kent 1959 AEC Regent V PFN858 which carried the livery of the associated Lockeys. It is posing for the camera at Toronto; happily this bus is now preserved retaining this livery. **8 June 1985**

LEFT: The reason OK Motor Services suggested a short ride to Toronto on East Kent PFN858 is evident in this view at Toronto where the road crosses a scenic valley. Various photographers wait further down the hill to capture the moment it crosses the bridge. **8 June 1985**

LEFT: The dome mounted fleetnumbers to allow roof mounted cameras in Chatham Pentagon to identify vehicles makes it equally easy to identify vehicles from a long distance. Former LT DM 1718 is now Maidstone & District 5024. It is parked between duties on the exit ramp. **31 August 1985**

BELOW: Turning the clock back a couple of months, we can compare the front of this East Kent Metroliner coach 8851 from the second batch with that from the first batch pictured earlier and it will be obvious that the angular profile has been softened. The coach is seen on Epsom Downs on Derby day. **5 June 1985**

ABOVE: Maidstone & District garage at Chatham (Luton) is the location of these two Leyland Leopard coaches on the left is 2545 which was formerly 4144 (UKR144S) and beside it is 4118 which would itself be renumbered to 2118 later in the year. **31 August 1985**

RIGHT: In 1980 Maidstone & District received five MCW Metrobuses for evaluation on behalf of NBC. Here 5267 stands in Chatham (Luton) garage. **31 August 1985**

ABOVE: This is P007 in the Maidstone & District service vehicle fleet. It had previously been 5007 in the operational fleet and pictured thus earlier. It is a 1969 Daimler Fleetline acquired from Northern General in 1972. Its new role is that of a recovery unit / mobile workshop area and as such operated on Trade Plates. It has been backed out of the workshop area at Chatham (Luton) garage for this photograph. **31 August 1985**

ABOVE RIGHT: Earlier in this book I illustrated the original 'black' Invictaway livery on a Leyland Atlantean. Here we see a revised livery version on Leyland Atlantean 5717 in Gillingham garage. **31 August 1985**

CENTRE RIGHT: Glass Canterbury Ltd had this all over advertisement painted onto East Kent ECW bodied Bristol VRT 7660 seen standing opposite Canterbury garage. **31 August 1985**

RIGHT: Canterbury garage yard finds East Kent ECW bodied Bristol VRT 7656 advertising National Holidays next to AEC Regent V training bus MFN948F (P192). **31 August 1985**

RIGHT: The reason for this long wheel base Leyland Olympian coach B446WKE, Maidstone & District 5446 being parked in Canterbury bus station is that it has been hired by The M&D and East Kent Bus Club for a tour. **31 August 1985**

BELOW: Being prepared for the long trip to Cardiff is East Kent 1974 AEC Reliance 6803FN in Canterbury bus station. This coach was previously registered PFN785M. **31 August 1985**

ABOVE: In 1985 East Kent operated a Sightseeing Tour of Canterbury. The vehicle selected was 7326 a former Southdown Daimler Fleetline seen here in Canterbury bus station. Note the unusual removal of parts of the upper deck side windows to allow passengers to take unobstructed photographs. **31 August 1985**

LEFT: Two Willowbrook bodied Bristol VRTs in the East Kent fleet wait between duties in Canterbury bus station. On the left is 7021 from the first batch and alongside is 7973 the first of the second batch. 7021 would see further service on Sightseeing work in London before being exported to USA where it operated tours in Chicago. It is now owned by students in New Orleans. **31 August 1985**

ABOVE LEFT: East Kent Berkhof Esprite bodied AEC Reliance 8205 which was new with a Duple Dominant body in 1973 as HFN55L is loading up in Canterbury bus station. Note the East Kent travel office signage behind. **31 August 1985**

ABOVE RIGHT: Somehow black bumpers rather than the white originals make this East Kent Leyland National appear dowdy. 1346 picks up passengers in Dover town centre. **31 August 1985**

CENTRE LEFT: Both Maidstone and District and East Kent received batches of ECW bodied Leyland Leopards in the 80s. Here East Kent example 8828 seen in Pencester Road Dover wearing local coach livery. **31 August 1985**

LEFT: Hoverspeed liveried East Kent Daimler Fleetline 7314 shares the Dover Pencester Road parking area with M&D Invictaway Olympian coach 5446. The Fleetline was acquired from Southdown in 1981. **31 August 1985**

UPPER LEFT: East Kent acquired eight 11m Leyland Nationals from London Country in 1984. Here the former LNB27 now East Kent 1127 rests at Pencester Road Dover. **31 August 1985**

UPPER RIGHT: From the first batch of Leyland Nationals delivered to East Kent in 1973 fleet number 1172 still looks smart in Folkestone bus station. **31 August 1985**

ABOVE LEFT: East Kent Leyland Leopard 8794 was originally registered PJG794S before receiving the current mark (6540FN) from a withdrawn AEC Reliance. It is parked in the corner of Folkestone garage with very little to identify it as an East Kent vehicle. **31 August 1985**

ABOVE RIGHT: Three of the re-bodied by Berkhof AEC Reliance coaches received National Holidays livery as illustrated here by 8198 inside the East Kent garage at Folkestone. **31 August 1985**

LEFT: At the time preserved by East Kent is this splendid 1956 Guy Arab IV with Park Royal body. Fortunately this bus survives in private preservation. The location is Ashford Station Road garage lower shed. **31 August 1985**

LEFT: East Kent trainer Leyland National P194 was from the first batch of Leyland Nationals delivered to Maidstone & District in 1973. It has been driven out from the lower shed at Ashford Station road garage for this photograph. **31 August 1985**